Poetic injustice

Bonnie's poetry captures the grit and resilience she saw in people during her many years of working as a police officer in Burlington. With dry wit and compassion she gives us a window into the day to day life of a police officer. Bonnie volunteered to work the toughest part of the city, showed residents respect, treated them with dignity and best exemplifies the ideals of "protect and serve." These poems are a treat to read. Anyone who has ever spent any time in police work will recognize a bit of their own experience.

— Lt. Emmet Helrich, retired

Bonnie has been writing poetry for the thirty years that I have known her. This is a wonderful collection. She has a special voice. Listen carefully.

— Robert Montgomery
Retired university professor

In Poetic Injustice *poet/cop Bonnie Beck brings to us the real life of a police officer on the beat, which turns out to be funny, heartbreaking, frustrating, nightmarish, and, most odd, loving. The encounters she describes with meth addicts, dealers, suicide corpses, families starving in heatless winter dumps, prostitutes, and various hustlers of all stripes, are rendered with unsentimental, muscular language—the poems breathe, they live. Again and again, coming in contact (as cops do) with people at the absolute worst moments of their lives, Beck does her legal duty cleanly and efficiently. But then she goes an extra step, buying gloves for the young thief released on a chilly winter day, slipping money to a prostitute who ends up calling her Pig on the street, ordering pizza for the family of a woman and her young children living in decadent poverty, remarking mildly to herself, "strange that you are picky about the toppings." It is a stark world, in which no good deed goes unpunished, and most of the action takes place at night, with "only sorrow in the sun." The fact that the poet can continue on with any sense of hope at all is miraculous. But, somehow, she does. The worlds of poet and police officer seem to be, in fact and in fiction, a cosmos apart. In these searing, vivid, moving poems Bonnie Beck unites worlds, like no other poet I know.*

— Jeffrey Skinner, Professor

Poetic injustice

Bonnie Beck

AMPress
Newfane, Vermont

Published by AMPress
A division of MarchMedia LLC
Newfane, Vermont

To order more copies, contact:
    AMPress LLC/MarchMedia LLC
    www.ArcherMayor.com

Designed and typeset by Kitty Werner, RSBPress

ISBN 978-0-9854276-9-6
1. Poetry. 2. Police-- Vermont-- poetry.
3. Vermont--poetry.

To Alana Ennis
who gave me my LE start in NC

Acknowledgments

I am especially grateful to Archer and Margot for treating my poems as precious, to my husband Rob who always has my back, my children Alyssa and Neil who have real grit and forever inspire me with their creative and loving spirits. Deepest thanks to my editor, Kitty for unfailing patience, compassion, guidance and encouragement

Bless the folks in the Old North End for their humor, respect and strength in adversity.

Thanks to Sheriff Don "sometimes you're the dog, sometimes you're the hydrant" Keeler who taught me how to shoot straight, and props to my brothers and sisters in blue at BPD. You can't make this stuff up.

Contents

Acknowledgments–|–8

Untimely–|–11

Policing the Range–|–12

Search Warrant–|–13

burn out–|–14

The Garrote–|–15

Path of Least Resistance–|–16

Done Deal–|–17

To the reporter–|–18

Snitch–|–19

Where do poems travel lost in cyberspace?–|–20

Back In–|–21

Equation–|–22

Rookie Rhyme–|–23

Evidence–|–24

A Street–|–25

Cyberbang–|–26

Lately I Ask Myself–|–27

Pick up stick family –|–28

Eviction–|–30

Dead Animal Dave–|–31

Interview Snippet–|–32

Vein of Gold–|–33

Daily Drama–|–34

The text said you knew–|–35

Bright St.–|–36

The Question–|–38

Christmas on Cedar Street–|–40

20 below blizzard–|–41

For T2–|–42

Rant # 67–|–43

Domestic–|–44

For Billy Joe Rayhill–|–45

Window Trail–|–46

The Bird in the Hannafords–|–47

Das Gluhwurmchen–|–48

For Frank Owen–|–50

Why Can't I Be Billy Collins?–|–51

Rio Bravo–|–52

Texas Nature Path–|–53

Gangsta–|–54

Mary–|–55

DIRECTV arrest–|–56

10·25–|–57

Clown Car–|–58

baited by the past–|–60

Mom's macular degeneration recipe–|–61

Shapeshifting in TX–|–62

Bartimaeus–|–63

The fur coat–|–64

About the Author–|–66

Untimely

Froth of maggots take your place
not the healing kind
Acidy death stinks and sticks to our uniforms
fills our nostrils thick with Vicks
On the phone with your daughter
you died peacefully
I lie
Watching the History Channel
in the tidy apartment
Neighbors thought him gone fishing
not scrawling notes
suicidal yearnings
 stuffed in a tackle box
by his side.

Policing the Range

Picking up brass this Autumn day
silent in our work
On the wide range
we chase catch
in hats and hands
cylindrical metal
hollows filled with dirt
spent treasures
Some dance on the grass
 hide under leaves
tinkling in cardboard boxes
In sun rain or snow
 we crawl collect
bend and sweat
Bullseyes staring in the distance
pistols quiet at our sides

Search Warrant

Cramped cold in the back of the tactical van
amidst the targets and bottled water
squeezed next to a jacket just like mine
He is strong as I lean against his arm
that does not budge
the ram is his
a shield is mine
This team of brothers
a line of blue
one hand upon another's
shoulder
stacked up
at the door
we stumble in
to crying babies
bad guys sleeping
needles, bags and money
an inventory of desperation
we haul back to the station

burn out

Never been to Montreal
not even Costco
Just stuck
 in the walls of this city jailed by
a job
tired of other peoples' drama
sunk in a hole
filled with nightmares
a Portage parvenue
 a palimpsest of the girl I
once knew

The Garrote

It did not make sense that knot
neither did the blood
the shaking dog at your head
contorted body on the kitchen floor
plastered hair on your blank eyes
Red footprints in the bathroom
red in the sink
Fear left
hanging
in every room we swept
He claims sanity
at court
His fleeting plea for
justice freedom
Your voice long silenced
by his rope.

Path of Least Resistance

Driving code to you
praying I don't kill someone along the way
I arrive heart pounding
 See you in the tub
filled with dirty water
Not quite floating
 in all your clothes
 holding a toaster above your head
 can't take it anymore
you cry
I picture you sparking and twisting in the current
Then I suddenly notice
the toaster's
 not plugged in

Done Deal

Locked in a cold hard cell

only I can flush your feces

only I can give you water

no blanket

no phone call to your gram

you

take off that belt, your shoes, those socks your
necklace

no chance to tell your side

then cuffed in my car now

never

maybe

free

To the reporter

Man Found Dead on a Frozen Grate the headline ran

drunk and homeless

You called him peter o tool when actually his name is
  Paul

Not caring enough to check that it was not the actor
  but

a complicated man

Stubborn his family said when I notified them

A silversmith and carpenter

His trades forgotten

washed away in a river of liquor

In your blurb on page 4

His life you documented

Printed as a waste

Snitch

Minions of swift
B
Dooly Cito
Friends from the city
left you in this seedy motel room
junked out and wasted
used up and worthless to everyone
except us
Even your mother, sister
brother I called
Oh, and your child
I wretched from your clutches
Crying, confused
took to the station
fed chips and soda
while you wired up
entwined in a buy.

Where do poems travel lost in cyberspace?

Do they float forever in some nebulous star cluster?
Burn brightly on their own?
Fall to earth on Christmas Eve as a miracle?
Like this one
A stranger from a fancy town enters her apartment
Sees the dog eaten furniture curtainless windows
drunk lazy sons and empty cupboards
In answer to an online plea to buy her freezer
he pays cash
leaves 50 gift cards in her mailbox
That night on a festive bus ride to walmart
visions of blenders swirl in her head
Christmas Day picture appears on my phone a
  raspberry chocolate milkshake she made
tied with a ribbon
A present to herself

Back In

Lying is an art form on this street
some talk too much
spill everything
since the ninth grade
claim their innocence
been clean 3 weeks doin good
Off probation
Maxed out
on the straight and narrow
Only a matter of time
like a fly resting by a swatter in my hand
chances are you won't survive
Your time cut short
out here

Equation

Take 2 lbs of pot
some guns and dirty laundry
Add
a girl scared of her shadow
Plus
an arrest in the dark
a car searched
Cops
toss bottles and diapers
toddler scrawlings
on the sally port floor
Pull out car seats once filled with dark-haired
    babies
that rode dirty with their daddy
Only sorrow in the sun.

Rookie Rhyme

dressed to perfection
can't make a decision
but shoots with precision
no sense of direction
asks all the wrong questions
arrests the poor victim
like a bird on first wing
knows not a damn thing

Evidence

Perimeter set
you're done
scared cornered thief
sorry not except got caught
fool
dropped your wallet at the crime scene
lays there open
a smiling you stares up
from your criminally suspended license

A Street

Cars drive dirty down it
stop at #50 for a buy
One gun two guns
Yard sale full of drugs
Ersatz street in the city
  Just an alley gone bad
For most a normal shortcut from a job
a quick ride through
two stop signs to t he highway
and you gone

Cyberbang

Gets a rush from stealin cars
beat downs
Facebook boasts build his cred
from a den of drugs
throwin signs
Street wise now walkin
talkin all tough
Once a child who
who leapt in my arms
No fear of me, nor hate of us
now sucks his teeth when I walk by
all menace and swagger
pretends he doesn't know me
his cold stare sears through me

Lately I Ask Myself

Why?

a crack whore calls me by my first name

arrested her so many times lost count

Why?

stay with that man who beats you

can't you stop ignoring your son for love of the needle

are you living in this maggot filled room

have two dogs and 9 puppies when you ask me for
   money for milk

Why?

are you stealing a mother's phone from her baby's
   carriage

jump on the back of a man from Nepal beat him
   senseless for no reason other than you are generally

angry

Why?

do you call me pig when I cut you a break so many
   times

Why?

Can't.I.sleep.

Pick up stick family

child
fierce and fearless
life you were born to
mother married your thieving step dad in jail
by phone
Last night you dreamed he killed her
cousin in next town
booting up
Father nearby visits
loves you and
the penne salad your great grama makes
She who raises you alone and teaches you to cook
made me a handwritten recipe book
when my own mother died
Now while your uncle

makes lists of stolen shirts

he tries to sell on the street

even to me

says

you are only a cop 10 hours right?

she endures radiation

tells me it has spread

throughout her long lived hard driven life

a soul's worth of sadness

pieces of it strewn

in a banner secretly sewn in his room

a Christmas gift from him

Eviction

Two little girls with straw colored hair

sit on a sheetless mattress

tears drip on the cold floor beneath it

From a dog eaten couch fast food bags stick out

Pit bulls claw to get out of the bedroom

where the drugs are

and the dealer sleeps

as the tenant whines,

*I pay my rent you gave me til the 24th I need
    somewheres to go dude!*

24th ended last nite at midnite, the sheriff replies. *It's
    one in the afternoon.*

Leave. Now.

The locks are changed

They straggle out in the frigid air

nothing in tow but a bundle of snowpanted babies

lucky what's left behind.

Dead Animal Dave

If on patrol you find a skunk
roadkill in the street
call city employee
Dead Animal Dave
to save these souls to keep
Maybe dressed in a robe having jumped out of bed
he judders down potholed roads
Drives the hearse with shovel and bag
he scoops
the bloody corpse
Takes it away to god knows where
A taxidermy lair?
some plot in the woods?
a sarcophagus ?
placed upon a pyre?
A roadkill cookoff
replete with his
squirrel base porridge?
Then one day I secretly followed
after he scraped up a lifeless lump
down a path familiar to many
the road to the local dump!

Interview Snippet

When' s a good time to talk to Jimmy?

Any morning between 7–8 am that's when he's sober

Why did you punch him?

He start a rumor my wife spread her wings for him

Oh.

You oughta citate him not me...and put an injunction on him!

And did your friend hold him down while you punched him? That makes him an accessory.

He didn't accessorize nobody!

How do you think I found out about this assault?

A monogamous caller?

So did you later come back and key his car?

No! I have an alimony! I was with my sister!

My.

Vein of Gold

An ostinato of street talk spills off the porch

*Yeah, girl got tired chasin it round the clock like a
  chicken with its head cut off*

Drawn to it she was

iron filings to a magnet

til now at death's door her life

riddled with track marks

a catastrophe of sorrow

carted off on a cot.

Daily Drama

Fell gunside hard
followed you limping
pleading
down one street
up another to Old Dump Road
vertical frozen path to the tracks
where you hiked down to die
Gave you money
for food and cigarettes
still you cried
Electric cutoff notice
Evicted
crack middlin boyfriend
back in
a baby no diapers
I see you
Crestfallen in the distance
cell phone to your ear
I call your name in the icy air
as you plod across the snowy field
A figure of dark
Despair

The text said you knew

he was down a one way street
behind a blue building
upstairs
Went there no answer
lights out
escaped
Wanted on warrants
   Wanted by you
to collect on a drug debt
  for your lover in jail
    begged you put money
  on his prison account
    like a child in Summer camp.

Bright St.

That giant deflating santa leans sideways in the yard
   of the shingled house

all

Winter

long

A casket warehouse stands empty next door to
   Bernadette's

Pictures of her favorite cops

taped on the window

facing out for us to see on patrol

Two doors down the house of unraveling relationships
   where you hide your stored skinny self

in the kitchen cupboard

beneath the sink

and won't come out

despite your mother's pleas

Knife to your throat weeping for your ex
a spectacle among the cans of soup
and lazy susan spices
We plead
then demand
Your hateful family
spews a background of curses
I just grab and pull
Now proned out on the linoleum
you spit on me
and whine
while your little brother
laughs.

The Question

just an argument about money, ociffer
I wouldn't hurt her
he slurs
sways in the threshhold
in the background she
shakes her head
points to a swollen lip her crying toddler
a room littered with broken wedding pictures
holes punched in the wall
smashed cell phone
probably caused
by
him
us
stuffed in the narrow
trailer park porch
fallen from

when Sarge latches on
in a cloud of pepper spray
rendered blind
we tumble
 bodies and tears
into the gnome filled
wind chimed
yard
onto the midnight sprinkler
pulsating
into the half full baby pool
decontaminating
us
him
why
don't you just leave ?

Christmas on Cedar Street

On patrol this holy night I see

your tree lists against the door unadorned topped
without a star

decorations abandoned at an old address empty crèche
at a snowy curb

Reminds me of your life

starless nights
tinseled with needles

lit with half burned bulbs
on a string of hopeless branches.

20 below blizzard

Dispatched here to your crooked wood frame building
son ripped off your rent money from the drawer
I exit my cozy cruiser into the wind
Up the icy sidewalk
use my hip to open your stuck door
at the top of 20 vertical stairs
Your stove is broke
Your kids are hungry
Heat is off
no tool on my belt will solve
no law on the books will ease your hunger
I reach for my cell phone and call
for pizza
I pay
strange that you are picky about the toppings

For T2

baker baker
you call me from holding
The Southern belle needs searched
so your wire does the job
in a world not known to many
a secret planet of pain
rotated by dollars
An orbit of chance
she buys for you
you pay up
he goes down
she is your satellite
your diamond in the sky
You
her only world.

Rant # 67

For the love of god how long will it go on you asking once again for money, food, bedclothes and pots and pans

this time

because your son and pregnant girlfriend moved out and took most everything leaving you and your pissant boyfriend with

nothing

but a shithole apartment and 3 pitbulls 5 puppies and in 2 days the sheriffs are coming to evict you

because you spent the rent money and now you are pregnant and need cash (even though you get checks every month for this and that) to abort a baby you cannot have at 42 due to your many health conditions and medications for ptsd and add and ppb and here's my new answer

so unlike my others til now.

gfy.

Domestic

In the shadow of Vesuvius
she stayed waiting for his wrath
exacting the time
his anger built
A first sign
the look in his eye
a shot across the bow
After days of sweetness and flowers
she stayed out late
no dinner ready
spent too much
Her life with him a lethal wheel
round with misery
I find her in a chair
sunglasses cover eyes petechiae
her voice gravelly from his strangle hold
she utters,
He tried to kill me.
Sits scared
her soul left diminished
his control
almost
complete.

For Billy Joe Rayhill

You said you would keep my love poems in one place

for posterity or maybe for your reading pleasure

perhaps a contest or secret public readings

Will you tuck them in a jewel box between rare
books?

Under a skimmer stone?

Buried by the Y shaped tree where we walk?

Under the cooking pot where you keep my birthday
cake?

Maybe memorize them to recite to me in the garden

or just nestle them in your heart where I sent them
from mine

Window Trail

Toss my ashes through the rocky window
slick rock under foot
stand on the precipice
bluest sky above you
beauty before you
my life swirled around you
my love enshrined forever in the view

The Bird in the Hannafords

I cannot concentrate on my grocery list for your
   endless chirp of

undeciphered songs

pleas for fledgling freedom born in the fake fig tree
   near the exotic fruits or

maybe tunes of happy delight scoring free food, a view
   of the sky and hibernation

At night do you come down from your skylight loft and
   swoop the aisles forage for seed

bang your fragile bones against the glass that keeps
   you from the starry skies?

Why not light on a shoulder or smuggle yourself out in
   the box of rotten fruit

Play dead in the cabbage?

Plan an escape plot with the plastic owls on the store
   roof

and their enemies the seagulls

that murder of crows in the nearby park.

Das Gluhwurmchen

I never heard when you told me

my eyebrows were my best feature

that God helps those who help themselves

turn the other cheek

you can't be all things to all people

stand up straight

smoking is a dirty habit

I thought you so old fashioned that you could speak
  Lithuanian and never wore pants

say the rosary in the middle of the day

scrub the floor on your hands and knees

Iron for hours

butter my father's toast each morning

now that my own wrinkles are set

I wish back that parcel of time to

hug you in the kitchen while you make chicken
  paprika

see your fingers fly across the keyboard

hear you sing glimmer glimmer!
beg for advice and opinion
let you plaite my pigtails with ribbon
and not complain
Learn how to cook and crochet
thanks comes too late for those
shopping trips and tin roof sundaes
soothing my own babies through hard times
a faith you so instilled
even now you must
in a heavenly pitch too high or low for me to hear
petition the nearby Saints
in a stressed holiness
please
help her
listen

For Frank Owen

Words like filigree brushstrokes on your canvas
These linear thoughts appear
without color
impressed quickly on an easel much
smaller than yours
A tiny page of
visible music

Why Can't I Be Billy Collins?

Sitting on the deck gazing out across the backyard
   planning to hint in a non nagging manner, I
   GUESS I'LL CUT THE GRASS!

long and waving in the breeze like wheat in your
   Uncle Jack's field

Chipmunks dash to and fro

A pileated woodpecker swings from the suet

Your head down, eyes closed book in hand

Never mind then about the mowing.

Instead I thank you for the delicious meatloaf you

made last night for dinner.

Rio Bravo

Impatient for the dawn

I sit in darkness

til the border roosters sing

a lone coyote barks on the river edge

sky silhouettes the ocatillos

mountains bright now

hoodoos in the distance

shaped like the hip of the naked woman in a painting
   that graces the near by bar

Texas Nature Path

Speed of light
Changes not
Nor this Juniper before me
number 7 sign at its trunk reminds
branches forever the same in all sorts of weather
today it shades with wings of green
graces a trail full of glorious light
a desert brocaded with flowers
Casts its weeping spell
Upon the tie down tree
And me who too remains
The same
Lost
off the trail
Not even cairns can guide my
Way

Gangsta

at the job

one more

picture posted warning wanna be on the street

a kid I gave some warm woolen gloves to last
   Christmas

left them with my card

now nods when he sees me

 stares out mostly from the stoop at 65

frownin at the po po

stylin on the steps in his red regalia

sagging his pants

on his sixty pounds soakin wet frame

22 in his waistband

soon to fall out maybe

pop him in the foot

lay him up

til he wakes up

before he's locked up

rockin orange

Mary

A voice in my dream echoed,
Salve Regina
chanted in Latin
a whispered promise
It will transform you
like snow upon a rock
My seedling faith
planted in soil of prayer
sprouted miracle
rustles my soul come Spring
an onion snow
dusts my heart with hope

DIRECTV arrest

There is a warrant out for your arrest
and because there is a warrant you try to hide
and when you hide
you get stupid
and when you get stupid
you let your girlfriend hide you
 in a big cloth zippered suitcase in the bedroom
and while you are in the suitcase
your girlfriend
sits on it
and because your girlfriend sits on it
the police think there is something in it
and since the police think there is something in it
they grab your girlfriend and she resists
and since she resists she gets cuffed
and when she is cuffed she kicks me
and when she kicks me
she gets lit up
tasered
50,000 volts
low amps

10–25

Meet me there
at North and North
before the end of midnight shift
sideways park in the rosy dawn
under the harvest moon
driver doors close up
mirrors barely touching
we share a story
like shot silk
a weft and warp thread of a thin blue line
a spooled love raveled back and forth

Clown Car

I picked up the comatose witnesses
from their hootch in the nearby woods
having warned them prior
you have to deliver!
please bathe in the river
refrain from the liquor for once!

Now stuffed in the back of my cruiser
the least of the foul up front
I rush to the trial with the stragglers in tow
up the stairs to the silent court
ALL RISE cried the bailiff
as my crew slowly did

stumbling up to the stand
one by one
spewed their story
what they saw that warm night

their buddy beat up on the shore of the lake
by the guy who now looks
contrite

Feeling much like a rock star
thinking this case is closed
the verdict's not guilty?

Then
the Judge leaned toward me
arms of his robe like
wings of a crow
in a whispered regard
   officer
   close by far
   but no cigar

baited by the past

3 months on the job I am
back in your bathroom
third time this week
  again you are beat up and bruised
  by your battering husband
  I am
distracted from your crying
by the bathtub full of swimming perch
  caught at the salmon hole
with the kids
who now 20 years later
  are grown
still
  casting out memories
  fishing most days
grief unfurled
same poles and bobbers and bathtub
still hooked by
  the relief of the river

Mom's macular degeneration recipe

Corn stuffing balls — best ever

½ cup chopped onions

1 cup chopped celery

½ cup water

1 cup chicken broth

1 can cream style corn

½ tsp pepper   ½ tsp salt

½ tsp poultry seasoning

3 eggs beaten

1 large loaf of bread· cut up

½ cup butter

Saute onion and celery in butter – until tender

add chicken broth, corn, salt and pepper.

Bring to boil – pour over bread

add eggs – shape into balls

place in pan – before baking pour on butter

Bake at 300 F for 20–30 minutes

Did I write to add 3 eggs????

Shapeshifting in TX

The paperboy's loud car muffler
wakes me daily in the East
but here in the sacred West
I soundly sleep
 chants and rain
clinks of burro bells
a Castenada dream
ends in the morning light
with a cactus planted
in a vase on the porch that was not there the day
  before
a lone dog trails me from my hike
tries to tell me something
runs in front of me turns to get my attention
I avoid
his green mysterious eyes
profundos ojos conocedores
mas puros que lose mios
 at the porch he sits by my side
so strangely loyal
looking for answers to questions
I don't know how to ask

Bartimaeus

How far can you run
how fast, to get away
you stay with neighbors, uncles, strangers
on porches, couches, floors
dressed in one filthy outfit
feral child
chunks of your hair missing
you pull to ease your pain
under a touk you hide at
age 11
seen and heard such horror
now, again
I find you asleep in a hallway
outside a schoolmate's door
In my cruiser we go to court
I'll not let you down this time, I promise
the judge puts you in another home
with another family
in a far away town in the mountains
where you flourish
in a loving embrace
a mercy deserved

The fur coat

in the salvation army window
 hangs
waiting
for a walk
to the corner store
once again
not looking out at the blustery day longingly
 but
snugly warming her
the one who dropped it off years ago
bored
maybe outgrew it
tired of winter
years it stays in that display

with the unwanted dresses

sad manikin coiffures

corduroy pants limped with time

no way to make them ever new

they all sag

those shirts pants and coats

  mourning their former owner

whose babies snuggled close to her breast

  against the striped cotton blouse

  a lover who wrapped an arm around her sweatered
  shoulder

nostalgia arranged in the window dressing

  memories for sale

About the Author

The author is a police officer in northern Vermont where she has been a patrol officer and recently a school resource officer. She won Honorable Mention in the TOP COP competition in Washington, D.C. in 2008 for her dedication to Community Policing.

Bonnie Beck grew up in Western Pennsylvania coal country with her four siblings above her family's funeral home. She graduated from the University of Pittsburgh at Johnstown and went onto Meredith College in NC where she student taught fourth grade.

As a police officer in Vermont, Bonnie was moved to write about her experiences as she worked with the residents on her beat. Since she has been writing poems since childhood, it was a natural to write about the life on the streets as she encountered it. Over the years, most of her poetry was long lost or given away, but after reading Jeffrey Skinner's book *The 6.5 Practices of Moderately Successful Poets: A Self-Help Memoir (The Writer's Studio)*, she decided to keep some.

Liked this book?
want to order more?
Contact MarchMedia at
Archermayor.com